This book belongs to:

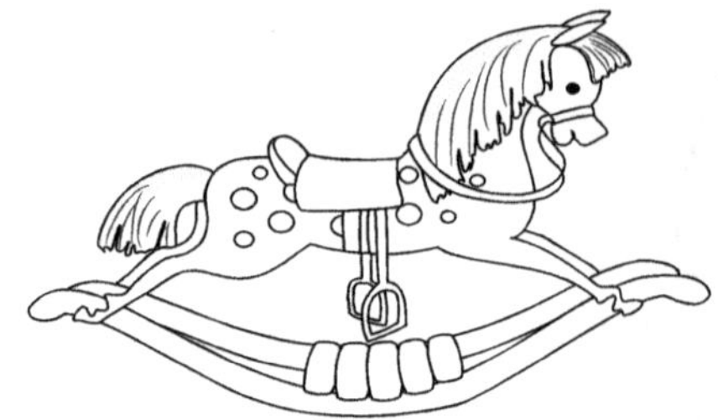

Merry Christmas!
To A Very Special Son
Coloring Card

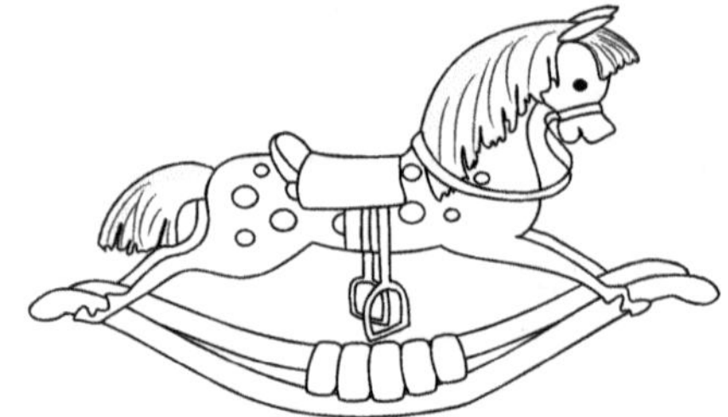

Joy to the world!

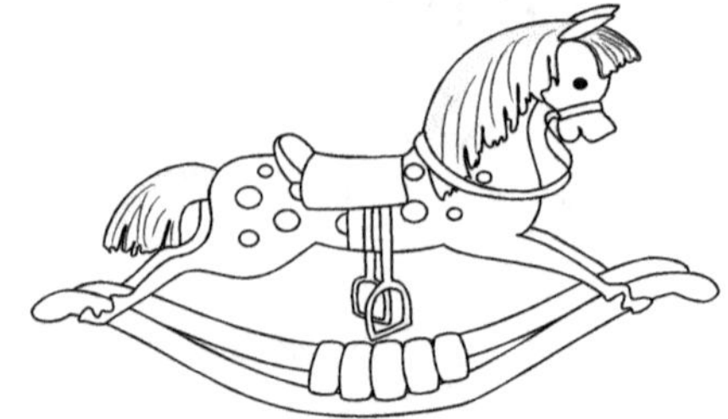

Warm wishes to you!

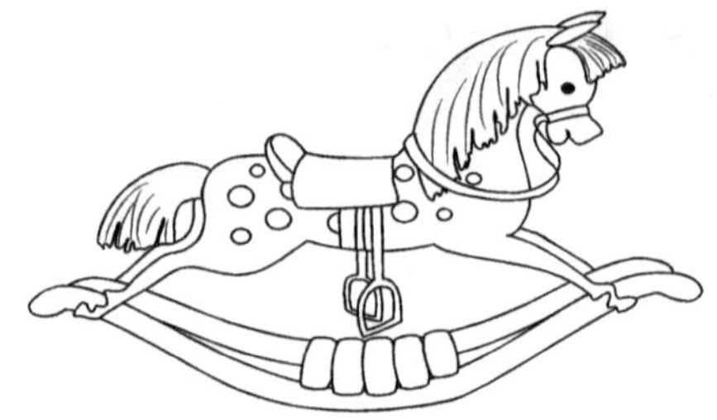

Merry and Bright!

Tis the season to be jolly,
fa la la la la la la la lamb!

It's the best Christmas ever!

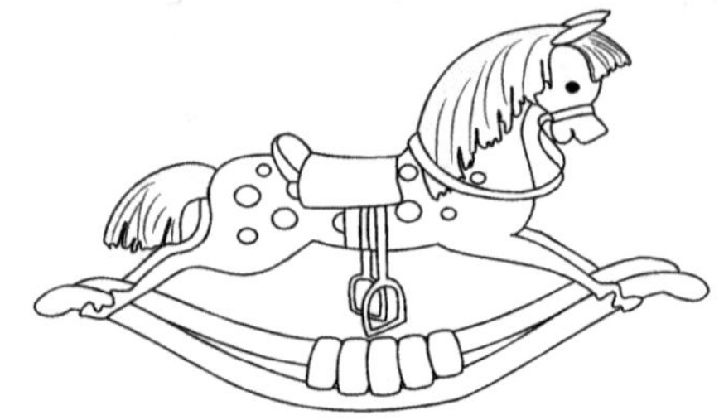

Joy to the animals!

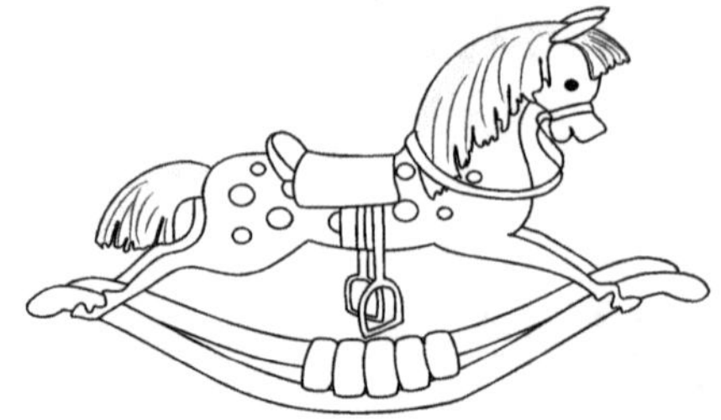

Santa's magic reindeer!

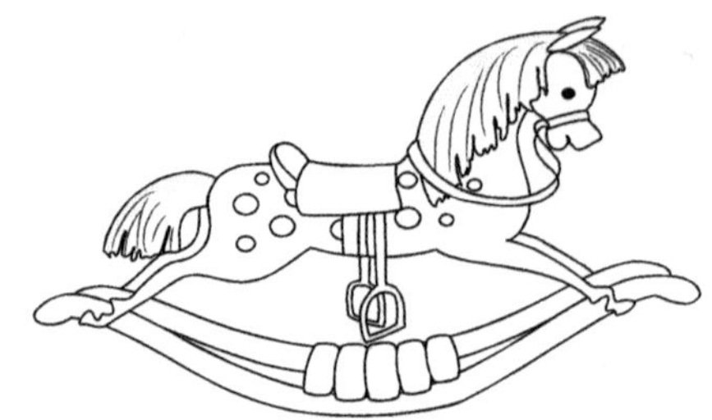

One of Santa's helpers!

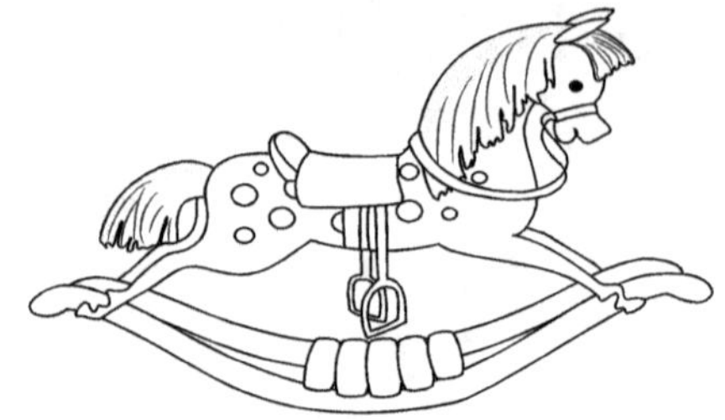

Flying in a winter wonderland!

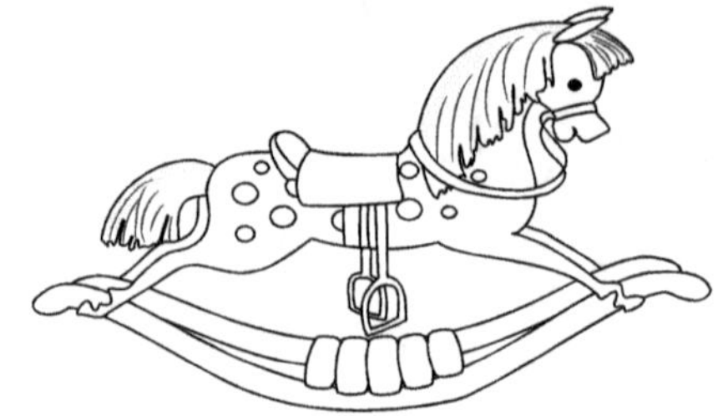

Merry Christmas
To A Very Special Son!
By Florabella Publishing, LLC